True Worth

How To Charge What You're Worth And Get It

By

Vanessa Ugatti
The True Worth Expert

First published in Great Britain by Solution Academy Limited in 2013. This edition published by HyperSuasion Consulting Ltd in 2015

Copyright © 2015 by Vanessa Ugatti

ISBN: 978-0-9937703-7-1 (Print edition)

ISBN: 978-0-9937703-8-8 (Kindle edition)

Contents

A Note On Grammar

As you read this book, I would like you to imagine that I am having a personal conversation with you. This means that, at times, there will be instances that won't be grammatically correct, for instance I know it's supposed to be 'to whom you sell' not 'who you sell to', but I would never say it that way if we were having a conversation; it's just too formal.

So while your old English teacher might have apoplexy at some of the things I've written, I hope you will understand why, and there is no need to email me about any grammatical mistakes you find (don't laugh – it happens!)

INTRODUCTION

With a sinking feeling, David checked his billings for the past month compared with his colleagues and wondered if the computer programme was on the blink. His earnings were barely higher than any of them and yet he'd easily spent double the amount of hours they had on client work over the past four weeks.

He thought of all the nights he'd been the only one in the office, staring bleary-eyed at his screen, hungry and tired but convinced the extra effort was going to be worth it.

Now, looking at his earnings, he knew it had not been worth it. It had hardly made any difference at all.

But what would make a difference? He knew that he couldn't put in even more hours or take on more clients. He didn't have the energy or the time.

All the extra tasks he did for his clients came to mind. "We trust you to look after us," more than a few had told him. But where had that got him really?

Despairing, David packed up his things and made his way out of the office. "Another six hours and I'll be back here," he thought, as he trudged towards the lift, wondering how he'd be able to face another month like the one he'd just finished.

I met David a few weeks later. By his own admission, if we hadn't started working together, he'd still be clocking up 80-hour weeks and never really making the money he deserved. He'd still be wondering what on earth he could do to improve his situation.

When David first rang to discuss working with me, he sounded like someone who'd completely run out of energy and enthusiasm. "I think I need your help," he said flatly. "I don't know what I'm doing wrong. I work really, really long hours but I'm not getting anywhere."

By the end of our first session, David had realised he didn't need to get more clients to earn more money or to work even longer hours. All he needed to do was to start charging his clients for the extra work he did.

Realising where he was going wrong was probably the easiest part of the process for David. Actually telling clients that he was going to be billing them for the additional work he did was, he said, one of the hardest things he'd ever had to do in his professional career.

But we worked on it until he was confident enough to do it. And it paid off. When he overcame his reluctance to tell his clients about charging them for the extra work they asked him to do, David made an additional £9000 in just three weeks!

What's more, in the year we worked together, he brought in an additional £46,000 by making sure he charged clients for everything he did. That still continues today.

The increase in earnings is just one of the things that have changed for David. He's no longer exhausted or devoid of energy and he's no longer the man who virtually lives at the office. Now, he's buzzing with ideas.

His voice crackles with energy and enthusiasm. "I'm a new man," he's told me more than once since that very first meeting.

In this book, I'd love to share all the techniques I give clients like David but there isn't enough space. Instead, I'm going to give you a few tips that you can immediately put into practice that will help you to charge what you deserve for your professional services.

You might be like David and not charging your clients for all the work you do. You might be discounting your normal rates to attract new clients or to keep existing ones. Or you might be charging less than you know you should for the work you do. Whatever you're doing or not doing, the result is that you're in a situation where the money you earn is nowhere near the value you deliver to your clients.

By the time you've finished reading this book, you'll know why clients resist paying you what you're worth and how to change that situation forever.

You'll know what to say and do to ensure your clients understand the value you bring to their organisation.

Most importantly, you'll feel confident about the value of your work and be able to charge what you deserve for the work you do.

The problem with undercharging is that not only do you lose out financially but you are in danger of becoming resentful towards your work and your clients.

You start to resent the time you have to spend working for your clients and you resent them for the demands they make on you.

They in turn quite often don't value the work you do or the extra things you do for them.

As a result, you feel under-appreciated and overworked and probably miserable.

That can change from today if you want. I am sure that by the time you've finished reading this book, you will feel a whole lot better about yourself, about your work and about your financial situation than you do right now. I know this because my clients tell me when they learn what you're about to learn that everything changes. Instead of "banging their heads against brick walls", things start to happen easily and effortlessly. Work, money, life—they all improve.

So, if you're ready to earn the money you deserve, let's get started...

UNDERSTAND THE VALUE OF WHAT YOU DO

To really get paid what you deserve for your work, you need to understand the value of the work you provide, then communicate that value to your prospective clients and finally be comfortable discussing your fees with them.

As a formula, it looks like this:

$$UV + CV + CD = CW$$

UV is understanding your value; **CV** is communicating your value; **CD** is being comfortable discussing fees and **CW** is charging what you're worth.

It's a simple formula but I know for many of the people I meet, it's also very challenging.

That's often because of self-worth. Our self-worth is at the heart of everything we do and it drives our behaviour. As human beings we are motivated by pleasure or by pain. So we're either moving towards pleasure or moving away from pain.

To put this into a business context, if you don't feel 100% worthy, how can you possibly charge what you're really worth? Your perception of what you're worth is too low.

If someone tells you to increase your charges, it makes you feel uncomfortable. When you feel uncomfortable, what do you do? You move away from whatever is causing that discomfort. So if the idea of charging more for your work makes you feel uncomfortable, you do whatever you can to get away from that thought or feeling. You stick with the fees that you're currently charging even if that means not getting paid what you deserve for the work you do.

Fortunately, there is a way to change the situation and it's one that won't make you feel at all uncomfortable. You're going to discover the value of the work you deliver. When you understand that, you will be able to communicate that value to prospective clients. That will help to boost your feelings of self-worth which in turn will enable you to charge what you're worth.

If you're like many people I meet, you might not really appreciate how valuable your work is to your existing clients or to prospective clients. You probably set your fees based on what other people in your market charge. Perhaps you heard that you should never be the cheapest or the most expensive in your market, so you set your fees somewhere between the two extremes.

You might also have conflicting beliefs about money. If you do, it's not surprising. Most of us are brought up hearing all kinds of opposing ideas about money. They probably include some of the following statements/beliefs:

- Money is the root of all evil. (The original quote is, in fact, "The love of money is the root of all evil." However, it is commonly misquoted.)
- Money doesn't grow on trees.
- A fool and his money are soon parted.

- Money makes the world go around.
- Money makes you happy.
- There is not enough money to go around.
- Men earn and women spend.
- I don't deserve to be rich.
- Time is money.
- Money is not spiritual.
- Money spoils you.
- Money is there to be spent.
- The rich get richer and the poor get poorer.
- I can't afford that.
- Rich people are greedy and selfish.

You might not even be aware of the fact that you have conflicting beliefs about money. Unfortunately, those beliefs will be influencing your behaviour. Your inner thoughts create your belief system, which in turn become your reality.

For instance, if you have a belief that 'money is the root of all evil', you will do what you can to avoid having too much money. If one of your beliefs is 'money spoils you', then you'll also do whatever you can to ensure that you don't have too much money.

Not all of the beliefs we have about money are negative. For example, I have always had the belief that I have plenty of money. As a result of that belief, I've constantly had a healthy bank balance and never once been overdrawn. It's such a strong belief for me that even when I was working part-time, I never had money problems. No matter how much money I spent, I always had plenty of money.

If you're struggling at the moment with money, I can almost guarantee that your beliefs about money are in conflict or completely negative. To change negative beliefs about money, you need to change your thoughts from negative to positive.

HOW TO CHANGE YOUR THOUGHTS

A quick way to change your negative thoughts about money into positive ones is to make a conscious effort to repeat positive affirmations throughout your day. Affirmations are statements that can condition your subconscious mind so that you develop a more positive perception: for example, of money.

Affirmations can help you to change harmful behaviours or accomplish goals, and they can also help undo the damage caused by negative thoughts; those things which we repeatedly tell ourselves (or which others repeatedly tell us) that may contribute to a negative perception of something.

Choose one of the following affirmations and repeat it throughout your waking hours:

- Money is good.
- I'm very capable of making lots of money.
- I deserve to make lots of money.
- It's OK to have more money than I need.
- I enjoy making lots of money.
- It feels good to earn money helping businesses succeed.
- Money makes life easier.

UNDERSTAND YOUR CLIENTS' NEEDS

To really appreciate the value of the work you do, you need to understand your clients' needs.

There's a difference between what Michael Port, author of *Book Yourself Solid*, calls your clients' 'urgent needs' and their 'compelling desires'[1]. Urgent needs, according to Port, are the things your clients feel they must solve immediately. These will be the things that have motivated them to make contact with you and hire you. Compelling desires are the things they want in the future.

How do you identify your clients' urgent needs?

You need to ask open-ended questions to find out what's going on with the client. Why is the client coming to you? What's the problem he or she is grappling with?

Open-ended questions are questions that can't be answered with a simple one-word answer while a close-ended question can be answered with a simple 'yes' or 'no'.

Open-ended questions begin with words like 'what', 'where', 'when', 'how', 'who' or 'why'.

---

[1] Port, Michael, '*Book Yourself Solid: The Fastest, Easiest, and Most Reliable System for Getting More Clients Than You Can Handle Even If You Hate Marketing and Selling*' (Second Edition), John Wiley & Sons, 2011

When you ask your clients open-ended questions, let them answer without interruptions, prompting or leading. When they finish speaking, you can then say "Tell me more about..." and "How...?" or a phrase like "Tell me about..."or "Tell me how..." or "Tell me why...".

Now, you probably won't ask a client "What's your pain? How much is this problem hurting you?" You wouldn't use the word 'pain' but that's in effect what you're doing; you're finding out what's causing them pain, although the words you use will be different.

You need to find out what it will mean to your prospective client to get the job done. What will it mean to them to overcome that problem, that challenge?

What will it mean if it doesn't get done? What will happen?

People use professionals because they have a problem that they need solving. You need to find out what solving the problem will be worth to them and what will the problem cost them if it's not resolved.

One of my clients, an accountant, charged his clients £175 an hour. Before he started working with me, he did a lot of work for clients that he didn't charge them for. Every time he did work for nothing, it was costing him £175 an hour. Obviously, that wasn't good for his business. It wasn't good for him either, because like many professionals, he had lots of internal conflict going on because he knew he should be charging for all the additional work.

What commonly happens is the following. One of your clients, who pays a fixed fee for a specific job to be done, say compliance work, telephones you and asks you to cast your eye over their cash flow forecast and let them know what you think. You say yes before you've even had a chance to think, or if you do think, it goes along the lines of the following: "Well I'm not actually doing any work (i.e. not creating the numbers), so I can't really charge them." And so you do it for nothing. You might spend half an hour or an hour doing it. Even if it's only half an hour, it adds up.

And what is that extra piece of work worth to your client? Is it saving them from making a mistake that could cost them thousands? Is it helping them get funding they would otherwise be refused?

And consider this. If it wasn't important to them, and if they didn't value your expertise and professional experience, they wouldn't ask you to do it for them, would they? Why waste your time and theirs on something they don't value? So, since it is important to them, and they do value you, they will be happy to pay for it.

Once you discover what your clients' problems are, it's important to reflect that information back to them. If you don't, they might not fully understand just how badly they want to have the problem resolved.

Learn to ask the same question in different ways to elicit the information you want. Find out what they want and then ask, "What will that mean to you when it's done?" Get them to focus on the benefit of using your services.

By doing so, you're helping them to see not just the features of your services but the benefits too. There's a difference between features and benefits that you have to communicate to your clients.

Features are what your services are. Benefits are what the features of your service mean to the client. Sometimes the benefits of your service will be tangible results and other times they will be intangible. They will be the impact your service has on your client's quality of life. Michael Port says benefits are "what make your offer an investable opportunity." They are the reasons your prospective clients will buy from you rather than your competitors. People buy results and the benefits of those results.

For example, if you tell a client, "I can do your compliance work for you" that's you describing a feature of your service. If you add, "That means you'll have more time to work on your business and do the things you're best at" you're describing the benefits that your service will provide. You're showing the client how your expertise will help them to save time and bring in more business.

Clients will probably not have thought of it in those terms. If you don't demonstrate the benefit of your services, clients will tend to see just the cost of hiring you.

If you don't first demonstrate the value of what you do, prospective clients are likely to regard the quote you give as high no matter what charges you offer.

You have to get them to shift from looking at your fees to seeing the value of your service. Once they understand the value, the fees you quote should actually seem relatively low by comparison.

If a prospective client asks me what I charge, I explain that I only work with people who I'm pretty sure I can help so that the return on investment is worthwhile. This means that I must have a meeting to find out if I can help them. Before I quote them a price, I make sure that they understand the value of what I will deliver. If they are ready for it, and they understand the value I provide, they will go for it.

If you don't establish the value, your fee will seem high and the value will seem low. Once you've created the value, the fee will seem low compared with the high value they'll be getting from your service.

It's really about you learning a new set of behaviours. To change any behaviour, you must first recognise what you're doing and why it's no longer working for you and then choose to do things differently. However, the behaviour can become so ingrained that you need someone like me to point out what you're doing and how doing things differently will improve your life.

I know from my clients how easy it is to get stuck in one kind of behaviour or one pattern of thinking and not realise how it's impacting their businesses or their lives. For instance, one of my clients seems very confident, but he's not confident at all. He's got it in his mind that he's boring because all he's ever heard from people outside the profession is that accountants are boring. I know that way of thinking has had an impact on how he conducts himself in business.

It's really important for you to realise that what you have to offer is incredibly valuable to your prospective clients. By hiring you, they can get on and do the things they're best at. You take care of the things that they are not capable of doing or they are not very good at doing. They can do the things they want to do because they know their business is in a safe pair of hands. You give them peace of mind and that is priceless!

Realising your worth is not about being big-headed, stand-offish or aloof. It's about understanding and appreciating your own value. It's about wanting to create that value for your clients, and charging what you're worth. It's about delivering a fantastic service to clients that other organisations or individuals probably don't deliver.

HOW TO DETERMINE WHAT MOTIVATES YOUR CLIENTS

People tend to be motivated either by the idea of moving towards what they want (pleasure) or moving away from what they want to avoid (pain). If the reward (pleasure) is big enough or the consequences (pain) are bad enough, people will be motivated to take action.

Now, some of your clients will be motivated by what they're going to achieve (towards pleasure) while others will be motivated by what they're going to get away from (pain).

For simplicity's sake, we'll call the people who are motivated by what they hope to achieve 'towards' people and the people who are motivated by what they hope to avoid 'away from' people. This matters because when you're talking about the benefits your service will provide, you want to motivate your clients to take action by hiring you. If you tell a 'towards' person that by hiring you, they can avoid feeling overwhelmed and stressed, they won't be that interested or excited. Tell them instead that by hiring you, they'll have more time to focus on getting new clients and they will be interested, because you've given them something they find motivating (towards pleasure).

To find out whether you're dealing with a 'towards' or 'away from' person, ask the following question:

- What do you want to achieve in your business?
- What's important to you about doing/having that?

An 'away from' person will respond with an answer that involves getting away from something, so you'll hear words like 'prevent', 'avoid', or 'remove'.

To motivate 'away from' people to take action, use words like:

- Avoid
- Exclude
- Fix
- Prohibit
- Stop
- Don't like

- Problem
- Steer clear of
- Solve
- Recognise

A 'towards' person will respond with an answer that involves moving towards something, so you'll hear words like 'get', 'achieve', or 'include'.

If you're dealing with 'towards' people, respond with language that will motivate them to take action. Use words like:

- Attain
- Gain
- Reach
- Goals
- Achieve
- Get
- Include
- Towards
- Accomplish
- Reward
- End result.

If you're not sure which kind of person you're dealing with and are not in a position to find out, use a combination of both motivators in your sentences. Talk about the pain of leaving the problem unresolved and the pleasure of achieving something because the problem is being dealt with.

VALUE YOURSELF

If you don't value yourself, how can you value your clients? How can you treat your clients well, if you don't know how to treat yourself in the right way? The more you value yourself and the more you charge what you're worth, the more likely you are to actually create value for your clients.

In fact, one client recently told me that since he's been charging what he's worth, he feels happier in himself and his creativity and performance are even better than they were before. This means that not only does the client get even greater value but he also has greater job satisfaction – a win/win situation.

HOW TO LEARN TO APPRECIATE YOURSELF

Here is an affirmation that will help to change your thinking about yourself and about the work you do for clients. It will help you to understand that you're creating tremendous value for your clients...

"I'm now creating fantastic value for my clients and in doing so I'm easily charging what my work is worth."

Copy this affirmation onto a piece of paper and repeat it throughout your day.

COMMUNICATING YOUR VALUE

When you tell clients your fee, or your hourly rate, you have to say it confidently. If you don't say it with confidence, your clients will pick up on your hesitation and doubt and won't accept it.

What should you do if you don't feel confident about your charges? You practise until you can quote them with absolute certainty and confidence, so that you are completely comfortable with them. You must be able to quote your charges with the same conviction that you'd tell someone it was a Monday or a Tuesday.

This applies to you whether you run your own business or work for other people. I know from some of my clients who work within large organisations that they don't always feel comfortable telling prospective clients the organisation's fee structure. I show them ways to learn to become completely confident about those fees so that before long they are able to tell every prospective client what the firm charges with complete confidence.

Here's one very simple technique to help you quote your charges with confidence...

Practise in front of a mirror. Look in the mirror and say, "I charge [your new fee]." Practise telling someone on the phone. Have a friend or colleague sit opposite you and practise looking at them saying how much you charge.

Keep doing it until you feel comfortable. Get comfortable with the sounds of the words. They are just words, nothing to be scared of.

When you practise with another person, make and maintain eye contact. Say it until your body and tone of voice are relaxed.

Have fun with it, don't take it too seriously. Before long, it won't seem like a big deal.

Right now the only thing that is really stopping you from charging the amount you deserve is the little voice in your head that's telling you it's too much. That little voice doesn't know what your clients will or won't pay; it really doesn't. Ignore the little voice. Prove it wrong.

I encouraged one of my clients to raise his consultancy fees by £25 an hour. For just one aspect of one piece of work which he was about to quote for, that would make a difference of £100 a month - £1,200 a year. And of course, it applies to every hour of work that he does, so the difference, in a year, would be thousands.

You have to consider not just the way you say things but how you say them. You need to feel certain that the value you are giving clients is so high that your fees are worth it. You must feel in your heart of hearts that the value you create for your clients is high. That takes away the feeling of "Oh, it's a lot to charge".

If you're an accountant, for example, think of the savings you're creating for your client; of how you're saving their company from making expensive mistakes or of paying more tax than it has to. You're going to be saving them money or hassle. You're saving them from non-compliance. You might be diagnosing what is stopping them from achieving what they want to achieve with the company whether that's poor cash flow, bad debts, late payments, spiralling costs, low productivity, under-investment, high wages, or something else.

Practising stating your fees will help you get to that point. I know that you might feel a bit silly at first but it's important you do this. The more comfortable you feel saying your fees, the more confident you will sound. Your prospective clients will hear the confidence in your voice and that will make them feel more comfortable too.   Remember, if you are the most expensive accountant or lawyer in your town or city, it probably also means that you are the best.

Now Go And Charge What You're Worth!

When you understand the value of what you do for your clients, can communicate that value to them and are comfortable discussing your fees, you will be able to charge what you're worth.

ABOUT VANESSA

The True Worth Expert.
Coach, Trainer, Speaker, Author and
Developer of the UV + CV + CD = CW Formula
to help professionals charge what they are truly worth

Vanessa Ugatti dramatically shifts the thinking for people in professional services taking them from their own perceptions of not feeling they can really charge what they are worth, to doing just that – and more! This unique ability, to bring out the best in people, has evolved for her over many years of facing similar challenges both professionally and personally, even questioning her own value in business.

With the development of her proprietary **UV + CV + CD = CW** formula, she works with professional services organisations and sole traders, instilling greater confidence and inspiring them to take the necessary action, resulting in incredibly fast changes that directly impact revenues and the bottom line.

She has always felt naturally drawn to understanding what it takes and how to make people shift. Vanessa has consistently challenged herself to experience the effects of her approach and methods and understand how a client feels. This helped her conquer many of her own fears and concerns, from dropping solo to work in a French-speaking part of Africa, launching a successful business later in life or overcoming a fear of heights by jumping out of a plane from 10,000 feet up!

The core value that drives Vanessa is authenticity; being true to herself. She finds this is the key approach to helping her clients be empowered to find their true selves and in turn their true value. This has led her to combine her more unique and some might say unorthodox way of being and be effective in industries that many would view as more conservative. She is by no means conservative. It works; some have even described her as Wonder Woman, with purple glasses, but the effect and results are still dramatic.

"I anticipate an additional income of £27,000 in the next 12 months."

Vanessa helped me understand and realise my true worth in the marketplace. I am now far more confident about asking for money and with the increase in my rates I anticipate an additional income of £27,000 in the next 12 months. I highly recommend Vanessa.

Ian Simmonds
Creative Director, The Big Bright Idea

When not helping others discover their value, Vanessa adds more value to her own life through a variety of action-based activities including spin classes, circuit training, dancing and dog walking. Maintaining her lifelong passion for the French language, but not their wine, she will be regularly found enjoying the cultural delights of her second country.

WHAT VANESSA'S CLIENTS SAY…

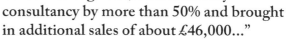

"In the year we worked together, I increased my consultancy by more than 50% and brought in additional sales of about £46,000…"

"I engaged Vanessa Ugatti to help me better understand my own value to my clients. As an accountant dealing with small businesses, I was sometimes afraid to charge for the advice that I was giving and therefore, on many occasions, completed work for free.

We built a framework for me to understand the clients' needs much better which then enabled me to communicate the benefits of the advice I was giving to my clients more effectively.

We also worked on strategies for spotting opportunities with clients so that these could be converted into tangible chargeable work.

In the year we worked together, I increased my own consultancy by more than 50% and brought in additional sales of about £46,000. There is no doubt that the work that Vanessa and I did together had a significant impact on the way that I operate and the fees that I am able to charge. The results speak for themselves. I wholeheartedly recommend Vanessa."

Roger Duckworth
Director, Ward Goodman Ltd.

"I can attribute at least £20,000 of extra turnover to the work that Vanessa has done with me."

"Vanessa quickly put me at ease and we proceeded, over a period of weeks, to look at the reasons behind my weak points and come up with exercises to help me overcome them. This included practical tasks as well as discussions.

The business quickly benefited and I can attribute at least £20,000 of extra turnover to the work that Vanessa has done with me. However, this is an on-going effect and I am continuing to make better use of my skills to bring in more work and profit to the business.

I shall be making further use of Vanessa's skills in the future and I have no hesitation in recommending her coaching to anyone who needs it but particularly to those who think they don't!"

Mike Cox
Managing Director, Open Sauce Systems Limited

"I have a fair and robust charging structure which has seen my income increase over a short space of time"

"I engaged Vanessa to help me create a charging structure within my business that truly reflects the value that I give to my clients. As a result I have a fair and robust charging structure which has seen my income increase over a short space of time, and which is continuing to grow. Importantly Vanessa is exceptional at holding up the mirror and making me personally accountable for my actions."

Jane Chamberlain
Business Owner, Censea Business Services

"I am now charging what I'm worth doing work that I want to do"

"Having worked with Vanessa, I am now charging what I'm worth doing work that I want to do. I feel more positive, less stressed and know that I can handle whatever happens in the business. I run the business; it no longer runs me. Vanessa is encouraging, very positive, optimistic, won't take no for an answer, dogged when she needs to be and focused. She is also very client-centred and doesn't allow the client to wallow, she keeps them looking forward with their eyes on the goal and how they will reach it. I highly recommend her."

Debbie Clark
Owner, Debbie Clark Consulting Ltd

"I am now back on track. My confidence has soared, I understand my value and am now charging what I'm worth"

"Before I met Vanessa, my confidence was a little dented, I was having difficulty attracting the right business and giving away far too much of my time for no return. After just 3-months' coaching, I am now back on track. My confidence has soared, I understand my value and am now charging what I'm worth. 2014 is set to be a fantastic year for me and the return on investment will be considerable. Vanessa is worth every penny and more."

Barry Blaker
Project Services Ltd

WORKING WITH VANESSA

Tired of working for a lot less than you're worth? Prepare to wake up!

If you've got this far, then the chances are that you recognise one of the problems Vanessa outlined, and you want to do something about it.

The first step to working with Vanessa is to request a complimentary True Worth Strategy Session.

In that session, you'll spend 30-60 minutes with Vanessa one-to-one, by Skype, phone or in person. You'll identify the blocks that are keeping you from charging as much as you could, and plan out a step-by-step strategy to overcome the blocks and charge your true worth.

To find out more, visit:

www.TheTrueWorthExpert.com/TWSS

or telephone: +44 1202 743961 or +44 7957 672335

or email: vanessa@thetrueworthexpert.com

Printed in Great Britain
by Amazon